1992

Doris:

This is for a very
special lady.

Love you

Red Pepper Paradise

Red Pepper Paradise

AVERY ISLAND, LOUISIANA

PHOTOGRAPHS BY A. J. MEEK
TEXT BY JO GULLEDGE
FOREWORD BY L. RONALD FORMAN

AUDUBON PARK PRESS
NEW ORLEANS, LOUISIANA

Copyright © 1986 by Audubon Park Press
All rights reserved
Printed in Singapore

DESIGNER: Joanna V. Hill
EDITOR: Martha L. Hall
TYPEFACE: Linotron Trump Medieval
TYPESETTER: G & S Typesetters
PRINTER: Toppan Printing Company, Singapore

LIBRARY OF CONGRESS CATALOGING
IN PUBLICATION DATA

Meek, A.J.
    Red pepper paradise, Avery Island, Louisiana

    1. Avery Island (La.)—Description—Views. 2. Natural
History—Louisiana—Avery Island—Pictorial works.
I. Gulledge, Jo.
II. Title.
F377.F57M44   1986   917.63'49   86-22353
ISBN 0-9616452-0-2

Contents

Foreword

Audubon Zoological Garden and Avery Island hold three goals in common: conservation, education, and recreation. Audubon Park also shares with Avery Island a place in the history books. Just as both command respect for their contributions in the past, so, too, are both committed to a purposeful future. It is, therefore, appropriate that a photographic essay on Avery Island should be selected as the second volume to be published by Audubon Park Press.

More than the headquarters for a multinational corporation, Avery Island, Louisiana, is home to untold numbers of flora and fauna. When the native egrets and herons were on the verge of extinction in the late 1800s, Edward Avery McIlhenny initiated the conservation efforts that have enabled them to multiply and flourish in the late 1900s. The plant life of the region was vastly increased and varied by the importation of specimens from around the world which could adapt to the marshlike terrain and the long hot summers. McIlhenny's interest in preserving natural wildlife habitats and their inhabitants was not merely a passing fancy; it became a life-long advocation that has been championed by his heirs. Avery Island is firmly ensconced in both the past and the future. The process of producing Tabasco sauce was developed there over one hundred years ago and has not been changed. At the same time, most of the acreage comprising Avery Island is a living trust for nature and will remain so for generations to come. Economics and ecology have met and demonstrated their ability to coexist. The natural resources of Avery Island have been kind to the McIlhennys, and that kindness has been reciprocated.

The public is welcome to share in the wonders of nature that are found in this niche of Cameron Parish. Visitors experience a peace and beauty not often found in twentieth-century urban centers. The senses of sight and smell are challenged by the unknown and unusual. Residents provide glimpses of a lifestyle not found in many areas.

We invite you to travel, via the photographic eye of A. J. Meek, to this south Louisiana community. Learn about the acclaimed conservation efforts of Edward Avery McIlhenny and his family. Relish the spectacular sight of fields of red peppers ready for harvest, the quiet majesty of a thirteen-hundred-year-old oak tree, and the rookery of snowy egrets. Meek has recorded more than images on film, he has captured a way of life that can serve as an example to the rest of us.

We are appreciative of the combined talents that have enabled us to share Avery Island with you. We extend our thanks to A. J. Meek for the photographs, which tell the story of Avery Island in a way that words cannot. Special gratitude goes to the heirs of Edward Avery McIlhenny for their cooperation in the publication of this work.

After you have had an opportunity to turn these pages, the Audubon Park Commission and the Friends of the Zoo know that you will agree with them that, just as Audubon Park is an Urban Eden, Avery Island is a Red Pepper Paradise.

L. RONALD FORMAN
Director, Audubon Park
and Zoological Garden

Photographer's Comments

A VISION SHARED

A typical south Louisiana hot and humid day marked my first visit to Avery Island. Crossing Bayou Petite Anse, I passed through the tollgate and went directly to tour the Tabasco sauce factory. After getting a view of the famous fiery hot sauce, I visited the Jungle Gardens. Later, sitting in the shade, I reflected upon the day's events. It was apparent that life moves slowly here: the Tabasco sauce waiting patiently in its oak casks; the alligators afloat, smiling; and the plants blossoming in the heavy air. I imagined time suspended; as long as I could sit here, be a part of the island, I would not grow a day older.

I made many visits thereafter to Avery Island, not to photograph, but to find refuge and to seek a regeneration of the spirit. Ultimately, I would go there to photograph, first in black and white and eventually in color. Color adds another dimension of understanding: a layer of information that is needed to convey the minute tonal qualities of sunlight and shade, the pastels of season—greens and pinks—all of which are invariably subtle in this region.

The island gave up its images slowly. I worked around the tourists visiting the gardens, excluding them in the camera's viewfinder. It was as if this place were a private Eden and the intrusion of people could interfere with the stillness, the serenity that exists there.

This quiet was abruptly interrupted one morning as I was startled by the crack of bamboo. A large buck leaped in his effort to avoid me. I remember how this graceful creature careened through the underbrush evading obstacles—ceramic olive jars and statues that decorate the Sunken Garden. It was a sight I did not record, because some moments, such as this, should be enjoyed and not photographed.

A photographer working with a 4 x 5 wooden field camera attracts curiosity and attention. As a result, I have often served as an unofficial guide to many of the island's attractions. The question most often asked has been, "Where are the alligators?" I finally realized what a European visitor was asking: "Can you tell me where I may find the 'ahh-*lig*-a-tors'?" I still smile when I think of it.

Trees and plants in the gardens have become as familiar as old friends. I have observed them through the seasons. Some have been lost to old age, many to frost, hurricanes, and other climatic conditions. I have been photographing there for three years, contending with heat, humidity, and hungry mosquitoes. I remember listening to the wind rustling in the trees while I was sheltered by the shadow of the hill and the dense jungle foliage. These memories remain rich.

These photographs are not intended to catalog plant specimens and wildlife but to share an artistic vision and to tell a story. That story is about stewardship, gentle traditions, and labors of love.

Red Pepper Paradise

2   Road and swamp of tupelo gum on south side of island

Red Pepper Paradise

AN INTRODUCTION

*In July all over the island when the peppers
bloomed you could smell the heat. . . . It was a
paradise of heat and moisture, no matter what
way you turned. Birds, egrets—what he called
water turkeys, gulls. The sky full if you shouted
across the water. Listen . . . go down to the water
and watch the bugs rising, the fish hitting at
them, the moonflowers opening for their single
night of blooming, the birds calling out of
sleep. . . . And the nutria and the muskrats
and the snakes . . . the whole island was alive.
The soil, the water, the trees, the plants in the
bayous—there wasn't anything at rest.*

John William Corrington
The Southern Reporter

Carefully cultivated fields of fiery pepper plants
burn scarlet in the July sun, and majestic cypresses and thirteen-hundred-year-old live oaks
form a softly shaded entrance into the world of
Avery Island. Within the exotic Jungle Gardens
we find lotuses imported from the Nile reflected
in shadow pools; sloping hills of Chinese timber
bamboo, and dense woods inhabited by deer and
black bear. Salt mines, among the largest in the
world, are located eleven hundred feet below the
island's surface.

Situated among the marshlands of south Louisiana, four miles from Vermilion Bay, which is in
the northernmost arc of the Gulf of Mexico, is
the unique geological formation of salt that is
Avery Island. Eight miles deep and six miles wide
across the visible dome, it is covered with only a
thin veneer of black soil in which the famous red
peppers for Tabasco sauce are grown. It is a rich
and verdant land that has supported the islanders
for well over a century. A hundred thousand
snowy egrets—one of dozens of varieties of birds
that make the island their home—build their
nests there, returning to the semitropical paradise
every spring in increased numbers. Special care of
the environment is a major concern of the people
of Avery Island, who have created and maintained
a culture quite different from those of nearby
Baton Rouge and New Orleans.

The history of the island is closely identified
with that of the Avery and McIlhenny families,
who have lived there since 1818 and have developed its natural resources of oil and salt. Although Avery Island is popularly known for the
piquant Tabasco pepper sauce, the salt mines,
leased and operated by the International Salt
Company, are the island's most lucrative com-
modity. Nearly 2 million tons of pure salt are
mined each year from the gleaming white tun-
nels. The oil industry, at peak nearly a hundred
producing wells, is a latecomer to the island
economy, its first successful production occur-
ring in 1942. Petroleum operations, confined un-
obtrusively to the western portion of the island,
have not disturbed the balance of nature. Opos-
sums, raccoons, and muskrats abound in the
surrounding marshes, protected from injury by
guardrails around the base of each well.

Early settlers, seeing the upthrust area in the
flat marshlands, called the salt dome an *island.*
Actually the oval-shaped hill, located several
miles inland from the Gulf, is a raised plug of
hard rock much larger than Mt. Everest, with a
core of pure salt. Only several hundred feet pro-
trude in a ratio comparable to the tip of an ice-
berg. Avery Island is one of five such formations
in the Gulf region. But the topography resembles
an island because it is surrounded by the waters
of the Bayou Petite Anse's curving fingerlike
streams. To the east, groves of cypresses loom
above the black-water bayou.

Over the centuries, the overflowing sediment
of the Mississippi has formed a connection to the
firmer terrain, over which runs the only road to
the island. The surrounding marshes (floating
prairies) are the habitat of muskrat, wild mink,
and nutria. Often referred to as the wonder island, five thousand acres teeming with life rise
152 feet above sea level, the highest point along
the Gulf Coast from Mexico to Florida. Although Avery Island is not considered a true island by geologists, Paul McIlhenny commented,
"It's an island because you can't step off without
getting your feet wet."

Located in the heart of the bayou country,
Avery Island has been regarded as a Garden of
Eden by generations of southern Louisianians.
For several decades, now, the wonders of the is-
land have brought tourists year-round to enjoy

3

the splendor and mystery of the Louisiana delta. The route to Avery Island, 150 miles due west of New Orleans, winds through rice and sugarcane fields, plantations, oil fields with derricks rising from the rich land, and through Louisiana towns that claim such titles as the Oyster Capital or the Gumbo Capital of the World. Signs dot the landscape featuring names such as Boudreaux and Fontenot, and three generations of families fish along roadsides or from flat pirogues settled in the black bayous.

The entrance to Avery Island, eight miles south of New Iberia, Louisiana, is marked by a small wooden tollgate that leads to winding gravel roads. Nearly 50,000 annual visitors enter the reclusive-looking world of exotic gardens and natural bird sanctuary built by Edward Avery McIlhenny through fifty years of patient nurturing. A visit here is an exploration into a microcosm of wonder and color. The surrounding grassy sea marshes reveal numerous varieties of turtles, alligators, and snakes, as well as nesting herons and egrets by the thousands. Fields of azaleas, camellias, and crape myrtles bloom each year in an array of brilliant color. Ironically, perhaps, Avery Island first came to national and international attention because of the famed Tabasco sauce. The pungent sauce with the bright diamond label has intrigued the tastes of millions for a century now. Acres of the scarlet peppers grown on the southern part of the island produce the ingredient for a product said to be copied but never duplicated.

But the history of the island is as colorful as the product it is best known for, and the story of the pepper's development and the discovery of salt (a necessary ingredient in the sauce) are inseparable. Salt was first discovered by accident on the island in 1790 when a young boy named John Hayes, out deer hunting, stopped for a drink from a briny spring. His family began bringing home bucketsful of the water to boil down for household salt. A plant for extracting salt was subsequently built at the spring's site during the War of 1812 by John Marsh of New Jersey, who obtained the rights through a Spanish land grant.

The plant was closed for a number of years but was revived and put into full operation during the Civil War. John Marsh's son-in-law, Judge Daniel D. Avery, for whom the island was named, donated salt to all the Confederate states. To keep up with demand he had to deepen the mine to thirteen feet, and at this depth workers discovered the first known pure layer of salt in the Western Hemisphere. But the salt, desperately needed by both the Union and Confederacy to preserve food, made the island a source of conflict. The Avery-McIlhenny families and the defeated Confederates were forced out, the operating buildings were burned, the salt mine was flooded, and the family sugar plantation, gardens, and natural preserves were devastated.

Following the war, the families returned to rebuild their homestead and to put the salt mines back into operation. The only thing to survive among the ruined herb gardens was a small defiant Capsicum pepper plant that Edmund McIlhenny had grown from seeds given to him by a friend passing through on his way from Mexico.

Experimenting with the pepper mash, salt from his own mine, and vinegar, Edmund McIlhenny developed the flavorful sauce and labeled it Tabasco, the name of the river and town in Mexico from which the peppers originally came. The word is also Indian for "land where the soil is humid," an appropriate description of Avery Island. By the 1900s the island was completely restored to its beauty, and the Avery-McIlhennys had established their salt-and-pepper fortune. The taste of Tabasco sauce, the growing of the peppers, and the production of the sauce remain the same after more than a century. Following the traditional method of preparation, the peppers are still picked by hand on the island, mashed, mixed with salt, and stored in barrels all in the same day. Nearly 10 percent of the peppers are grown on Avery Island; the rest are grown in Honduras, Mexico, Colombia, and Venezuela, protection in case a hurricane destroys the island's crop.

Generations have hallowed the island's ways but none so much as Edward Avery McIlhenny, who was born there in 1872 and who spent his boyhood roaming the rich and plentiful wilderness that surrounded him. After his graduation from Lehigh University, "Ned" McIlhenny, a naturalist, joined Admiral Peary's Arctic exploration in 1893 to study migratory birds. He continued his explorations, financing an expedition to Alaska. After years of global travel as a naturalist, hunter, and fisherman, he returned to his home to find that most of the wildlife had vanished. The greatest loss to him was the disappearance of the egrets and herons, whose plumage had gone to the milliners of Paris and New York. Because of the great demand for their spectacular feathers, the birds were nearly extinct.

In the spring of 1892 McIlhenny collected seven young, starving snowy egrets from the island's marshes. He built an enormous flight cage over the artificial Willow Pond and watched the egrets build their own nests to raise their young. Setting them free during the migratory season, McIlhenny allowed the birds to join flocks heading to South America, and was thrilled to see them return the next year in increased numbers. Owing to McIlhenny's initial care and the continued conservation efforts of the family, each spring more than 100,000 egrets return to Avery Island's Bird City, along with a variety of ducks, geese, herons, *poules d'eau* (coots), and blue ibises. E. A. McIlhenny is considered one of the earliest recognized conservationists in the United States.

As spectacular as the island's Bird City is the two-hundred-acre Jungle Gardens, redolent of rare flowers, plants, and trees that McIlhenny brought from countless verdant places of the earth. Designed to gain the ultimate effects of color and harmony, the garden has 30,000 azaleas—white, many shades of pink, red, and purple—which come to full bloom in early spring; 17,000 varieties of irises; and 65 kinds of bamboo. The world-renowned camellias, comprising 400 varieties from Asia and Europe alone, are bordered by desert palms. Astonishing displays of multicolored wisterias from the Orient drape the branches of the native live oaks alongside giant red daisies from Central Africa.

To the original acreage, the family added surrounding property to total eighteen square miles, most of which is still kept as natural wildlife habitat. Nearly 700 residents of Avery Island, most of them workers in salt and Tabasco production, enjoy comfortable coexistence with the island's wildlife. The island community, nearly self-sufficient with its own school, stores, post office, and homes, continues to emphasize the conservation efforts that have been maintained for nearly one hundred years. At Avery Island visitors can experience an unusual harmony among people, industry, and wildlife flourishing in one small world.

Looking east toward New Iberia

Western view from hilltop

Pickers at harvest

Looking east across pepper fields

Tollgate, Avery Island

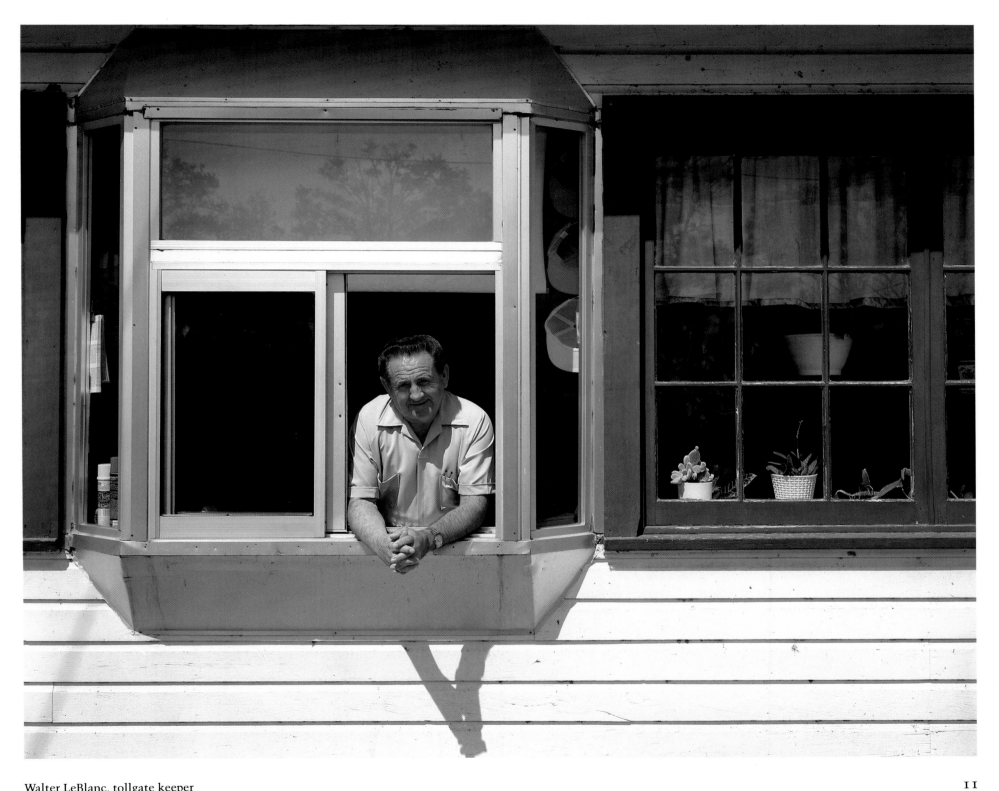

Walter LeBlanc, tollgate keeper

12

Oak, McIlhenny Company offices, and original Tabasco
sauce factory

Mr. Raymond Labit at Avery Island store

View of main road and International Salt Company,
facing south

International Salt Company

Oak tree and salt company housing

Salt company and community

Cedar tree and salt company village

Residence of Mrs. Eola Richard

Underground, International Salt Company

Underground, International Salt Company

Wisteria and commissary

Mrs. Eula Mae Dore at work in commissary

Christmas tree, an Avery Island tradition

First light, Avery Island

Oak and pepper fields

Tabasco Sauce

Peppers, salt, and vinegar—the ingredients in the spicy Tabasco sauce are simple, yet the pungent taste is a culinary experience matched only by its aroma. Although modern methods are used in manufacturing the sauce, the basic process has not changed since Edmund McIlhenny concocted the flavor in his own kitchen, following the Civil War, to enhance the bland food available in the Reconstruction South. The peppers are still carefully cultivated in the black topsoil and mixed with Avery Island's own salt. There are no secret ingredients that make this a special product; it is simply the result of a longstanding pride in quality.

New pepper seedlings, sprouted from the previous season's more hardy selections of ripened pods, are transplanted by hand from the rows of greenhouses and hotbeds to fields in early spring when the chance of frost has passed. Each full-grown plant produces thousands of pods, which change from green to yellow to a brilliant crimson by harvesttime from late July to October. The picking, which continues six days a week during the peak season, is completed by 3 o'clock in the afternoon. Although mechanical pickers have been experimented with, only the expert hand of experience can distinguish between the ripe pepper and the perfectly ripe pepper. Workers, mostly islanders or local people from New Iberia, gather on the oak-shaded headland—ridges between the fields—to cash in their boxes of peppers for payment by the pound. The laughing and bantering continues in English, but more in Cajun-French patois still spoken by descendants of early settlers from Nova Scotia. The selection of the valuable pods for seeds, the weighing of each bushel, and the cash transactions are all handled by members of the McIlhenny family, following in a century of tradition.

The trucks, filled with the hand-selected peppers, travel the short distance from the southern section of the island to the factory. A crusher grinds the fresh pods into a mixture of eight pounds of salt to every hundred pounds of Capsicum peppers. The mash is then funneled into four-hundred-pound-capacity Kentucky-oak barrels, like those used for wine, for three to four years of aging. The barrels are sealed with wooden lids that are drilled with holes to allow gas to escape; the lids are coated with a thick layer of salt, and the long fermentation process begins. The aroma of the concentrated pepper mash is an eye-burning experience for the visitor unfamiliar with hot peppers.

The aged slurry is mixed with vinegar to stand for another month and is continually turned by wooden paddles during every working hour. Each barrel is personally inspected by a McIlhenny for true color, texture, and aroma. Only then is the filtered sauce piped to the next building to be bottled and packaged in the familiar red and green box for distribution. Each section in the newest factory, built in 1980, is separated by a system of air locks so the powerful aroma does not affect the bottling and warehouse area. All interior structures, even of the new facilities, are constructed of wood to prevent corrosion by the powerful vinegar fumes. The remaining seed is dried and sold as a by-product used to make candies, cinnamon gum, and oil of Capsicum. The Avery Island factory, along with quality-controlled bottling plants in Caracas, Madrid, Montreal, London, and Mexico City, produce 187,000 bottles a day or 50 million of the two-ounce size every year. With 125 international markets, Japan surpasses all other countries outside the United States with annual sales of 6 million bottles, followed by Canada, England, Spain, France, Italy, and West Germany. In 1973 the McIlhenny Company expanded its line to include Tabasco Bloody Mary Mix, packaged in Illinois.

Tabasco pepper sauce, often called Cajun Catsup, has been a success ever since Edmund McIlhenny strained the condiment into household jars to give to family and favorite friends. So enthusiastic were all who tasted the sauce that McIlhenny sent his entire inventory, packaged in ladies' perfume bottles made by a local glassmaker, to 350 wholesalers in 1868. One year later he received thousands of orders at one dollar a bottle, and the sauce was patented in 1870. A London office was established in 1872 to handle the overwhelming orders from Europe alone. The bright red, white, and green diamond-shaped label, bearing the McIlhenny name, became what is now one of the most widely recognized emblems around the world. The original corked bottle with green sealing wax soon changed to a metal cap with a splash of bright green foil at the neck in 1882. The sauce received a gold medal for excellence at the World's Industrial and Cotton Centennial Exposition in 1884–1885 held in New Orleans.

Upon the death of Edmund McIlhenny in 1890, responsibility for the family-owned business went to his son John McIlhenny. A graduate of Harvard, he promoted the product using current marketing techniques, including advertising campaigns. He participated in food exhibits, featuring the savory sauce; displayed the trademark and bottle on posters and walking-billboards; and gave away thousands of miniature bottles of the pepper sauce—a practice still popular with visitors who tour the Avery Island factory. John McIlhenny changed the company name from E. McIlhenny to E. McIlhenny Sons in 1895. After he was appointed a U.S. Civil Service Commissioner in 1906, the company's operations then passed to his brothers Edward Avery (Ned) and Rufus McIlhenny. In addition to overseeing the daily operations of the factory, Ned McIlhenny spent his life developing the island's Jungle Gardens and Bird City. Rufus McIlhenny, with a degree in engineering, handled Tabasco sauce production problems, purchased supplies, and traveled throughout the eastern United States investigating the possible advantages of installing automatic filling and labeling machinery, until then all done by hand. From 1868 until 1910 the family bottled the pepper sauce in the family "laboratory." Then the old building was replaced by a new factory built to accommodate the latest technology and handle the increasing demands for the product. This factory was used for seventy years.

Without changing the production method of the sauce, Walter Stauffer McIlhenny, son of John McIlhenny, again modernized the factory in the 1940s by installing newer bottling equipment and 2000-gallon vats for processing. He hired an advertising company and encouraged modern market techniques.

Under Walter's presidency, until his death in 1985 when Ned Simmons was elected to the position, the company's annual sales increased 10 percent with a growing market in foreign countries accounting for nearly 40 percent of the total. But the rough-textured walls and wooden equipment necessary for Tabasco's unique flavor have remained, following McIlhenny Company's philosophy: "Don't change anything that you don't have to." In 1980 the company expanded operations on the island with the completion of a larger and more modern facility located on the site of an old pepper field. In a time of overwhelming fast-food production, the family-owned company has steadfastly rejected purchase offers from conglomerates. It continues the deliberately aged quality product in small quantities, the Tabasco Pepper Sauce that still titillates palates after 125 years.

Oak leaves and pepper fields in late summer

Young pepper plants in March

Willie Dore, field supervisor, in greenhouse

Exterior of greenhouse

Harry Brook, truck driver, and Calvin Benjamin, helper,
take pepper plants to fields

33

34 Planting peppers in April

Cultivating pepper plants in late spring

Rows of pepper plants in early summer

Pepper plants and early morning mist in late summer

Entrance to new Tabasco sauce factory

New Tabasco sauce factory

Aged pepper mash

Pepper mash aging with salt covering oak barrels

Dave Landry, Tabasco sauce shipping supervisor

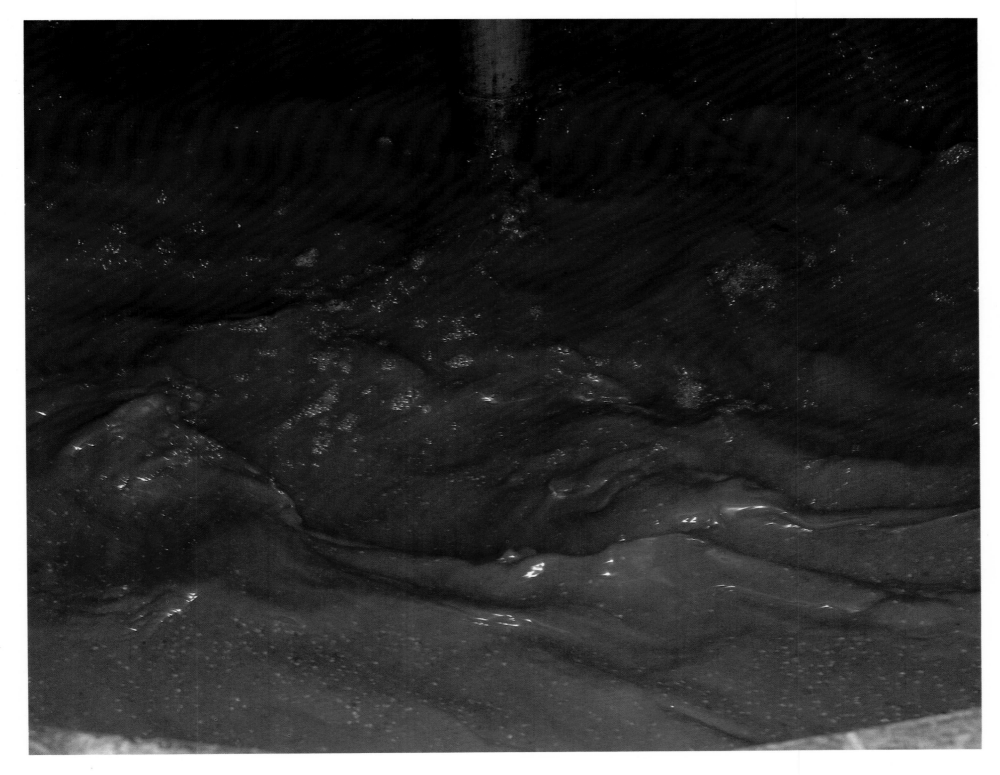

Tabasco sauce in mixing vat

Joseph Sam, Tabasco sauce factory worker

Louisiana's Eden

THE JUNGLE GARDENS AND BIRD CITY

Edward Avery McIlhenny often said to visitors, "I am building and planning for the future. I may not live to enjoy the completed picture, but my children and grandchildren will." Not only do his descendants enjoy Ned McIlhenny's works, but fifty thousand visitors cross the little road each year to marvel at the fruition of his visions.

He never stopped developing the estate during his lifetime, and the gardens' cultivations and developments have been continued by his heirs since his death in 1949. These heirs and other members of the McIlhenny families have continued to protect the island's natural resources and wildlife.

Among the giant native live oaks and pines, Ned McIlhenny—conservationist, naturalist, writer, explorer, businessman—planted gigantic timber bamboo, papyrus, Japanese magnolias in a natural woodland setting. He converted the raw marshlands into what area residents refer to as Louisiana's Garden of Eden—a small world of natural and manmade wonders for the public's enjoyment. Unusually beautiful animal specimens live in the harmonious, exotic gardens. White-tail deer feed on the grasses and roam the lush green forest; alligators glide through the bayous; and snowy egrets sail overhead in search of food for their young.

Visitors, who pay a nominal charge at the garden's entrance, make their way through thick vegetation that looks much like the upper regions of the Amazon jungles, with miles of roads and footpaths on two hundred acres. The original entrance at the stone archway has been replaced by a visitors' center, where guests can stop and pick up a map that includes a brief history of the gardens. Visitors are immediately enveloped in the serene atmosphere of man and wildlife existing together, where emphasis is on maintaining the environment. They will see the deer, so tame that they stop to watch passersby, and the egrets that nest across the road from the busy Tabasco sauce factory. Most guests drive through the gardens, but a more enjoyable tour is by foot, discovering the hidden paths paved with footstones. Acres of azaleas, the most abundant flowering plant in the garden, cluster in vibrant springtime color among stately magnolias, which open their great white blooms in late spring and early summer.

Although every season in the Jungle Gardens is unique, spring brings color at its most dazzling. From February to late April, thirty thousand azaleas, sprawling giants and border dwarfs, in single and ruffled blooms of red, pink, magenta, white, and lavender, a hundred varieties or more, cast a rosy florescence over the island. At peak blooming the foliage of the evergreen shrubs disappears under the brilliance of the flowers. No visitor, particularly one from a cold climate, can ever forget the early spring display on the subtropical Avery Island.

Toward the end of summer glossy hedges of Oriental hollies, which border the garden roads, begin to show their red berries; and early autumn's colors follow in the hues of chrysanthemums—bronze, yellow, white, red, and lavender.

During the usually mild winter, from late November to March, the island again comes to new life, this season with its world-famous collection of the camellia japonica. Many of the eight hundred varieties have been imported from France or from their native China or Japan. The porcelain-perfect flowers grow in a profusion of reds, pinks, whites, and a great number of variegated specimens against the dark waxy foliage of large and shapely shrubs. A popular species in the collection is the camellia susanqua, usually smaller and with pink, red, and white flowers, less showy but with a quality not found in the camellia japonica; the susanqua has a delicate fragrance.

Transcendent to all the seasonal beauty of the Jungle Gardens are the thirteen-hundred-year-old live oaks, considered to be the finest in existence. Their great branches of fine evergreen foliage spread out from massive trunks to offer fields of shade, most welcome to visitors during summer's heat.

Among the most charming sights of the island is the centrally located Chinese Garden, where the solemn antique Buddha sits staring into the dense foliage from his glass temple. The Buddha idol, created for the Shonfa Temple during the reign of Emperor Hui-Tsung (A.D. 1110–1125), was a gift to Ned McIlhenny from friends who found it at a New York museum. The near-six-foot statue is covered with a fine dusting of gold and capped with a conical toque studded with lapis lazuli. Sitting on his sacred lotus, he rests in a clearing of live oaks interspersed with groves of giant Chinese timber bamboo. An artificial lagoon, nearly six hundred feet long, meanders beneath the arching oak limbs that shade clumps and drifts of delicately tinted Chinese irises on the bank. Seven sacred hills of the Buddha surround him, the crown of each twenty-foot mound planted with varieties of Chinese azaleas. Around the base of each hill, borders of Chinese junipers and double rows of Chinese camellias complete the careful pattern. The Chinese Garden is a serene and lasting home for the Buddha, which students of Oriental antiquity have said is the finest to come to America.

Not far from the Chinese Garden, a three-hundred-foot shadow pool, between rows of live oaks, reflects clusters of Chinese wisterias, vertical clusters of sweet flowers in shades of white, pink, and lavender. The heavy vines of giant wisteria from Japan entwine to make an arbor of lavender during spring, a fragrant tunnel alive with bumblebees. In still another section of the garden, McIlhenny blasted out an entire hillside in order to plant various palms, giving the effect of a desert in the middle of an oasis.

Near the center of the garden sixty-foot canes of Chinese timber bamboo grow. Nearly sixty-five varieties, including laceleaf fern bamboo and Titan timber cane bamboo, are found throughout the gardens. During the warmest season, one variety has been found to grow more than an inch during the daylight hours between 8 A.M. and 5 P.M.

Among seventeen thousand varieties of irises, species from Siberia can be found along with plants from all parts of the Northern Hemisphere. Set in a garden half a mile long, the irises, delicate of form and color, are in full bloom from March to late April.

The iris gardens and bamboo thickets surround the giant sanctuary, Bird City, which houses tens of thousands of snowy egrets and numerous other kinds of birds, including the purple gallinule. More platforms have been constructed each year since Ned McIlhenny set his endangered snowy egrets free that first season in 1892. They return every spring after spending the winter in Central and South America. During the mating season, from late March until mid-July, Willow Pond is supplied with truckloads of twigs and branches brought in for nesting materials. The thirty-five-acre pond is an almost solid mass of white—American and snowy egrets, and white herons, intermingled with such birds of colored plumage as the glossy black ibis, the scarlet tanager, the anhinga (snakebird), and the great blue heron.

Perhaps the most moving and spectacular sight on the island, one near the heart and vision of Ned McIlhenny, is the great flocks of snowy egrets as they fill the skies over the gardens and gracefully come to rest at their home on Avery Island.

Oak grove

Japanese magnolia and Spanish moss

Azaleas, late blooms

Oak grove

Spanish moss on oaks, eastern border of garden

Cycad, winter frost, first crossroads

Decaying tree trunk, oak grove

White azaleas, entrance to long lagoon

Shadows in summer, long lagoon

Late afternoon, long lagoon

Long lagoon

Pond, second crossroads

Moon rising, long lagoon

65

Oak arch near Bayou Petite Anse

Moon rising, long lagoon

Cypress trees in fall colors

Woods across from second crossroads pond

Cypress trees, second crossroads pond

Wisteria and fallen oak, second crossroads

Spanish moss, long lagoon in late afternoon

Spanish moss, long lagoon at noon

73

Wisteria, pond, and azaleas between Woods Circle road
and long lagoon

Wisteria, pond, azaleas

Sunset at long lagoon

Buddha's temple in late afternoon

Buddha

Buddha's overlook at sunset

Gnarled cedar and view of Buddha's temple

Cedar branches, Buddha's lagoon

82

Marsh grasses near the seven hills

Alligator, west lagoon

84

Yucca in bloom

Crape myrtle, west lagoon

Holly hedge and Wisteria Arch

Holly in winter bloom

88

Oaks, bamboo, and vines near Wisteria Arch

Woods near Wisteria Arch

Near Wisteria Arch

Fallen blossoms and shadows, Wisteria Arch garden

Wisteria Arch in summer

Wisteria blooms under arch

Chinese tallow tree, Palm Garden

Overlooking Palm Garden

Oaks, azaleas, overlooking woods near Palm Garden

Oak, from the Palm Garden

Tree arch, overlooking Bird City

Fallen tree, Bird City

Egrets nesting, Bird City

Egrets nesting, from observation tower, Bird City

Marsh plants along shore of Bird City lake

Egrets nesting, from observation tower, Bird City

Oaks and azaleas, near Camellia Garden No. 2

Grove and azaleas, near Camellia Garden No.2

Olive jar, Sunken Garden

The Sunken Garden

108

Yuccas in bloom, center forked road

The Sunken Garden

Camellias

Camellias along Woods Circle road

Broken palm trunk and golden bamboo, Woods Circle
road

Camellias along Woods Circle road

Broken palm trunk and golden bamboo, Woods Circle road

Bamboo, Woods Circle road

Japanese magnolia, Woods Circle road

Fringe tree, Woods Circle road

Azaleas in Camellia Study Garden

Azaleas in Camellia Study Garden

118

Magnolia in Camellia Study Garden